New American Style

NEW AMERICAN STYLE

foreword by
SUZANNE SLESIN
design editor
CONDÉ NAST
House&Garden

MIKE STROHL

PBC INTERNATIONAL, INC.

Distributor to the book trade in the United States and Canada
Rizzoli International Publications Inc.
through St. Martin's Press
175 Fifth Avenue
New York, NY 10010

Distributor to the art trade in the United States and Canada
PBC International, Inc.
One School Street
Glen Cove, NY 11542

Distributor throughout the rest of the world
Hearst Books International
1350 Avenue of the Americas
New York, NY 10019

Library of Congress Cataloging-in-Publication Data
Strohl, Mike.
    New American Style / by Mike Strohl
        p. cm.
    Includes index.
    ISBN 0-86636-537-0 (hardcover). — ISBN 0-86636-512-5 (pbk.). —
    ISBN 0-86636-511-7 (international hardcover). —
    ISBN 0-86636-510-9 (international pbk.)
    1. Interior decoration — United States — History — 20th century.
    I. Title.
NK2004.S76 1997   97-22488
747.213—dc21   CIP

CAVEAT—Information in this text is believed accurate, and will pose no
problem for the student or casual reader. However, the author was often
constrained by information contained in signed release forms, information
that could have been in error or not included at all. Any misinformation
(or lack of information) is the result of failure in these attestations. The
author has done whatever is possible to insure accuracy.

10 9 8 7 6 5 4 3 2 1

Printed in Hong Kong

To Karen Fisher
for her example,
inspiration, and
support.

CONTENTS

FOREWORD

There's no question that things are happening in American decorating — not that it was ever really quiet on that front. Interior design seems to have evolved from rarefied "interior decorating is only for a few" to the more informal, and entertaining approach of "interior decorating as a quasi-national pastime."

We are now in a period of style and taste revolution. And we are obsessed with decorating. At cocktail parties from Atlanta to Seattle, at sit-down dinners on Fifth Avenue in Manhattan, or by the pools of Bel Air mansions in Los Angeles, talk turns swiftly from real estate to drapery styles and the price of upholstery. With the help, speed and variety of media today, our sense of style is being influenced by a multitude of forces. People respond to it all, take it home, and integrate it into their lives. Passion, fantasy and a reinterpretation of the past come into play.

The big names in decorating still count. But so do the immense talents of the current roster of designers who are quickly becoming new household names. They have been and are continuing to be in demand not only because of their individual styles but because of their clients. Instead of seeing their clients as creative road blocks, designers are accepting and feeling challenged by unusual demands. They are also finding themselves changed by the process. Their projects and their clients' homes reflect an openness to the exciting world out there. The exotic lives comfortably with the familiar. Furnishings from India, Thailand, Paris and Istanbul either shipped back or found around the corner add to the mix of Eastern and Western cultures. Flea market finds and museum quality antiques. Eclecticism and minimalism. Spareness with soul. Welcome to decorating for the millennium.

Suzanne Slesin
design editor
CONDÉ NAST
House & Garden

INTRODUCTION

A revolution in home design is sweeping America, offering each of us new opportunities and freedom of style that were unthinkable a generation ago.

Since interior design came into its own in the early part of the twentieth century, it seemed that there were trends. Now there are no trends that anyone takes seriously. In the 1980s, in fact, a number of adventuresome interior designers began offering their clients an informal approach to decorating that the clients had largely developed for themselves. Frames suddenly didn't need to have pictures or mirrors in them. Stacks of books became worthy design elements. Priceless antiques were often paired with pieces of unknown heritage rescued from the street. Mismatched collections of dining room chairs became quite acceptable. Industrial furnishings and architectural antiques next to moderne? Why not? "New American Style" had arrived—and it is continuing to evolve.

America has been called many things, but perhaps the most apt description is that the country is a vast melting pot, or salad bowl. So many elements are assembled in this country, so many cultures are represented, that the mix has become America's identifying character. The freedom to blend—old and new, formal and informal, hard and soft, witty and serious, bold and calm—has been embraced wholeheartedly by designers from Kennebunkport to Kauai, and adopted by designers around the world.

Evident in the projects featured, moreover, is that most American of traits: an inherent practicality. The design textbooks have been shelved and the style rules have been rethought to capture individual personalities and express a particular point of view, even if that means a mixed message. Honesty has become the best policy in today's home design—a revolutionary spirit which is, above all, true to individual expression.

Mike Strohl

Leslie Harris Interior Designer ∞ **Tim Street-Porter** Photographer

A NEW CONTEXT

Southwestern California • 1,800 square feet/167 square meters • design budget: not disclosed

Most people travel with baggage. It's no surprise that when residences change, most or all of one's possessions, which may have looked spectacular in a previous residence, need to be repositioned within the new context.

Designer Leslie Harris became an editor of sorts at Weepah Way, a compact, stucco-clad, stripped-down, two-story Spanish bungalow in California. The owner, an avid collector of antiques, bric-a-brac, religious art, kilims, and very fine antiques enlisted her to bring some order to his varied collection of furnishings and decorative objects when he relocated himself and his belongings from an Italian-style villa to these more modest quarters.

A type of recycling took place — very little remodeling was done, with only a few new furnishings. For instance, what was once a dining room table now serves as a desk. Two small bathrooms were combined to make a more ample one, and a storage area was refigured as an enormous walk-in closet. Much of the interior effects were achieved with paint, and by highlighting the existing moldings, wooden ceilings and beams, and other existing architectural elements. Harris designed wooden grids that were installed over a number of windows and doorways, which provide enough privacy and tailoring so that curtains were not deemed necessary.

There is an inherent sense of minimalism within all the rooms. While an eclectic array of objects and furniture pieces are positioned and displayed, there's seemingly no clutter and each item is given enough breathing room to be shown off to its best advantage. Brightly colored objects are strategically placed for balance. The color of the library alcove's walls is daring, and gives the area a separate character from the main living space.

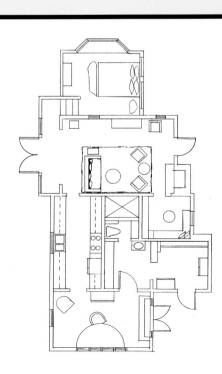

"I truly believe that if you buy good, timeless pieces in traditional sizes that they should be able to work in any home," says Leslie Harris, the designer of Weepah Way. "I have never believed that what the house looks like on the outside should determine what furnishings should look like."

Celeste B. Cooper ASID Interior Designer   ✛   **Richard Mandelkorn** Photographer

BOSTON UNCOMMON

Boston, Massachusetts • 2,500 square feet/232 square meters • design budget: not disclosed

A Zen look can be achieved without the monastic implications. In the case of a Boston residence with interiors designed by Celeste B. Cooper, a comfortable feeling is presented in a "cool as a cucumber," fairly monotone environment. Pattern and texture are accorded primary status. Also of prime importance are shape and scale, and the interrelationships of the individual pieces, all selected for their strong, simple lines and exquisite quality.

It's not as if the rooms are unnatural or inhumane: there is a value placed on natural surfaces, natural patinas, and stark, eye-popping contrasts that aren't overwhelming. Tranquil, yes, but not drowsy. The eye is directed toward intriguing placements and groupings, where lines converge or create patterns of their own against the sand-colored background.

Black is used sparingly as an accent, a recurring element that adds focus to a room. In keeping with the spare aesthetic, windows feature rice-paper pull-up shades, or nothing at all, keeping light levels even, while allowing for glimpses of the ever-changing vistas of the Charles River just outside.

Designer Celeste Cooper purposefully avoided the use of too much detail, allowed textures to create pattern, and made a strongly graphic statement without verging on the pretentious in this Boston residence overlooking the Charles River. Modern classics mix with new elements harmoniously in a gallery-like setting that exudes a natural warmth through selected organic elements interspersed throughout.

Matthew P. Smyth Interior Designer ■■ **Peter Margonelli** Photographer

REVISED TRADITION

Upstate New York • 1,250 square feet/116 square meters • design budget: not disclosed

The simple clapboard village house in the Hudson River Valley serves as interior designer Matthew P. Smyth's weekend retreat. His goal in decorating the house was "to blend, but not to match" the "careful mix of periods and styles," which were selected to complement one another and create an overall sense of relaxation.

Smyth set up distinctive contrasts through-out the house where textures and patterns abound. When glazed cotton confronts leather, for example, or when geometric patterns are positioned close to solids, the result is a pleasing and eye-catching mélange. Basic wools, cottons, and linens were selected for upholstery, "to highlight the shape and design of the piece," explains Smyth, who used one floral-print chintz on a sofa to set it all off.

Colors throughout the interior are "soft and soothing," according to Smyth, and show off the forms of the juxtaposed American, English, and Continental furniture and objects that were bought at flea markets, country antique shows and auctions, or are hand-me-down family pieces. The mix represents a fresh approach to traditional design, which Smyth feels is a very new American concept.

23

Patterns and textures play off of one another in Smyth's highly personalized rooms. Simple wooden blinds are found on most windows, some of which are left uncovered to show off original tracery. The living room windows are attired more traditionally, yet in a clean and spare manner. Most seating pieces were selected for comfort as well as looks.

Antique hickory floorboards were recycled for use as kitchen countertops. A country-style ambiance is created through selected styles of furnishings, which convey a sense of true Americana.

The baronial-style English Tudor bed is an inspired choice within the context of this modest house. Designer Matthew Smyth chose to update and downplay its drama by discarding the traditional hangings for a simple linen canopy. Although the rooms are not overly cute or sentimental, a nostalgia for simpler times reigns throughout.

Ronald Bricke Interior Designer **Michael L. Hill** Photographer

MIXED METAPHORS

Paris, France • 650 square feet/60 square meters • design budget: $65,000

The envelope is utterly French: a Louis XV-style flat in the heart of the romantic, historic, and very chic Marais district on Paris's Right Bank. But Manhattan-based designer Ronald Bricke approached the design of this studio apartment pied-à-terre in a fashion that is far from typical.

Instead of following the traditional route, filling the main living/dining/sleeping chamber with formal brocade-covered fauteuils and bergères, bureau plats, bombé chests, and other period pieces, he embraced the style born in Paris in the 1920s — Art Deco — for a bit of a twist as well as for practicality. The color scheme is light, bright, and monochromatic, combating any sense of crowdedness. It makes for a thoroughly modern and freshly inviting space.

Bricke carefully and selectively combed a Paris flea market — the Marché aux Puces — to find the perfect combination of furnishings, lighting fixtures, and decorative objects. They were chosen for scale, simplicity of line, multifunction (screens, headboard, and footboard are all storage areas, but do not broadcast the fact), and for high-style impact, without appearing too stiff or fussy.

31

Animal-skin rugs are scattered over the fine wood floors of the space, adding a further touch of informality to the architecturally imposing setting. All light is filtered through sandblasted glass or white alabaster for a luminous ambiance. According to Bricke, the choice of furniture, its arrangement, and the color palette employed "give a great sense of size and space to what is essentially a one-room apartment."

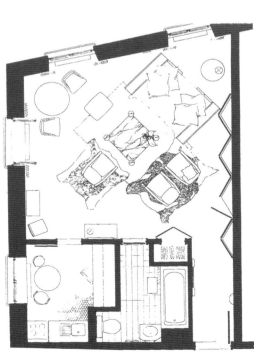

CUSINA

Jill Sharp Interior Designer Rob Brinson Photographer

GETTING PERSONAL

Atlanta, Georgia • 500 square feet/46 square meters • design budget: $5,000

"Simplicity: it is how we live now — The Gap, Banana Republic, natural fibers and materials, four-wheel-drive Jeeps, Dean & Deluca, cashmere sweater sets — with fewer but far better quality possessions," explains designer Jill Sharp. Designed on a frugal budget, her apartment in Atlanta does not seem to be the kind of place one would find in a 500-unit apartment complex, but it is. The richly textured space speaks of an individual with a distinct eye.

"Objects and furnishings that catch my eye and somehow feel familiar to me mix together to make a style that just says me," she says. While the modest-sized apartment is filled to the brim, it is not congested. "Being limited to a large main room with an attached galley kitchen and one bedroom, one bath, space is paramount!," exclaims Sharp. "I use the living room as one undivided space, whereas most people delineate a dining area and a living area. A coat closet accommodates my hundreds of magazines, and a stacked pair of Chinese wicker laundry baskets brims with fabrics."

Contributing to the airiness is the color scheme: "Color in my home is reduced to various shades of linens, whites, and silver, with punches of red and green. I use lots of leopard-print fabric and piles of ticking as color blocks," Sharp remarks.

Everything is lovingly positioned, and no matter how small the item in the collage, it is still of great significance.

Every element in designer Jill Sharp's Atlanta apartment has personal meaning, from the piles of fabric she collects, to the signage lettering she uses in lieu of artwork, to the black pencil-post bed that she says will always be with her "despite the fact that it's a squeaker."

José Solis Betancourt/Paul M. Sherrill Interior Designers ■■ Andrew Lautman Photographer

A STEP BACK

Washington, D.C. • 294 square feet/27 square meters • design budget: $50,000

Spareness mixed with drama leaves the cold to the outdoors in a Washington, D.C. sitting room mindfully composed by interior designers José Solis Betancourt and Paul M. Sherrill of the Solis Betancourt firm. Each element within the room scheme "has a strength of its own without overpowering its neighbors," explains Sherrill, describing the not-too-precious, soothingly comfortable atmosphere they created.

Light and airy fabrics are joined by lush and sumptuous chenilles. The ripple-folded gauze window treatments "refract an ethereal light," according to Sherrill, who believes this, in turn, assists in communicating an appropriate kind of intimacy in the space. Contemporary slim-lined furniture pieces which don't turn their backs on tradition are key, as is the strategic placement of denser, rougher forms offset by wispier, sleeker ones. Colors are rich and subtle, with patterns introduced in a precise, tailored way.

Art pieces and decorative objects are used to "add texture and depth," says Sherrill. "Personal items are a must, as they speak of who lives there."

The crisply rendered sitting room is full of soothing confrontations that give the space an especially rich depth. Comfort is not forgotten, with furniture selected for its look as well as its feel, and pieces arranged for interaction as well as appearance.

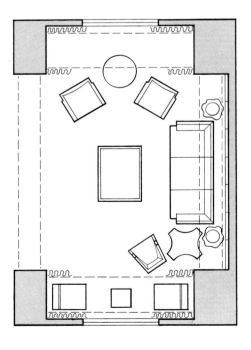

Mike Strohl Design Publicist   **Peter Margonelli** Photographer

URBAN HOMESTEAD

Metropolitan New York • 600 square feet/56 square meters • design budget: $50,000

There's no need to be afraid of history in New York City, where unpretentious city digs combine a number of styles and periods to create a dynamic and imaginative fusion. The country comes comfortably to the city, with warm, familiar furnishings blended into an urban milieu. The mixture includes pieces depicting a diversity of materials and surface effects, from marble and iron to decorative painted pieces. High-style design statements with a capital "D" confront more traditional, romantic items. There is a kaleidoscopic quality to the décor, but the positioning and restraint of the design keep the effect clean and graceful rather than jumbled.

Throughout the apartment, the walls are painted in rich, bold tones. Strong colors are not feared, but rather create a sure sense of place in each room. Extensive collections, including modern and contemporary paintings, sculpture, posters, prints, and ceramics, as well as the silhouettes of the furnishings, are clearly set off in a graphic and appealing way.

It's clearly not Kansas, but a contemporary take on the homespun incorporated into this show and tell space reflecting a distinct personality and aesthetically diverse interests.

The farmhouse comes to the metropolis in this one-bedroom apartment. There is a country flavoring to the spaces, but little room for sentimentality. Each space is multifunctional, with the living room serving as a dining space and guest room, and the bedroom performing quadruple duty as a TV room, den, and library.

Richly colored walls are covered with an extensive collection of paintings and photographs acquired at flea markets and galleries. Incorporated into the mix are furnishings rescued from city streets and restored.

Sig Bergamin Architect/Interior Designer ✤ **Tuca Reinés** Photographer

High Impact

São Paulo, Brazil • 775 square feet/72 square meters • design budget: $90,000

Making a statement with color isn't so simple. The color-charged São Paulo living room conceived by interior designer Sig Bergamin, who divides his time between firms in both New York City and Brazil, is carefully orchestrated and balanced. "Most people are afraid of brights," says Bergamin. "Colors don't need explanations or justifications, they are beautiful in their essence," he adds. Within a room he describes as cosmopolitan and designed for entertaining, he demonstrates that a rainbow of colorful elements can be used in concert to create a stunning, extremely lively, and very urban impression.

A kind of Pop-Art sensibility is at work, one that appreciates the rich impact of colors and the harmonious relationships that can be developed by placing them together. Styles of furniture from a variety of periods that might seemingly clash, gently collide instead in a tour-de-force fashion, with a solid color applied to each piece setting it apart within the composition. Most important to the designer is the quality of the form of each individual piece. Wood-paneled walls serve to warm up the space and provide a natural, cozy frame for the electric dialogue taking place within.

49

"I was not preoccupied with the idea of anything matching," says Sig Bergamin of the color-rich living room. The eclectic collection of furniture includes mostly classic French pieces from the nineteenth and twentieth centuries. They are positioned atop a bold, Matisse-inspired rug, which seems to hold the composition together. A rich range of fabrics, including velvets, silks, taffetas, damasks, and leather, add texture.

Annie Kelly Interior Designer ■ **Tim Street-Porter** Photographer

CINÉMA VÉRITÉ

Los Angeles, California • 3,000 square feet/279 square meters • design budget: not disclosed

This Los Angeles house, built in the 1920s, has a glamorous history. The Mediterranean-style villa in the Whitley Heights section of the Hollywood Hills was always attractive to designer and artist Annie Kelly and her husband, noted architectural photographer Tim Street-Porter. Both British-born, they left London for Los Angeles over twenty-five years ago, intrigued by the fantasy of Hollywood and its architecture.

They've created their own version of fantasy in this house, called the Villa Vallombrosa. It was designed by architect Nathan Coleman for Eleanor de Witt, an easterner who wintered in California. "As an antiquarian, she filled the house with antiques and tapestries bought on annual trips to Europe," says Kelly. Though the property was divided after de Witt's death in the 1950s and various changes were made, Kelly and Street-Porter were determined to recapture the romantic style established by de Witt: "A nostalgic sense of old Europe with period furniture, wall hangings, and textiles," states Kelly.

The palazzo atmosphere of the house is enhanced by the selection of furnishings, mostly Italian antiques, but not totally limited in provenance. While a certain period is evoked, the strength of the design program is in the wealth of textural effects, the mingling of formal and informal elements, and the inclusion of personal artifacts.

53

The Villa Vallombrosa was lovingly
restored and decorated by designer
Annie Kelly to capture the spirit of its
original resident, an antiquarian who
spent winters in Los Angeles from the
1920s to the 1950s. In keeping with
the style of the house, Fortuny fabric is
used throughout and the majority of
the furnishings purchased are originally
from Italy, though elements from a
range of cultures assist in re-creating
the image originally fixed by de Witt.

Friends provided a number of valuable objects included in the redecoration of the Villa Vallombrosa. Artist and decorator Tony Duquette contributed smoke-patinated dining chairs, rescued from a San Francisco museum fire, which Kelly reupholstered in Fortuny fabric. A narrow shelf along the perimeter of the room is used to display an extensive collection of Chinese porcelains. A comfortable, lighter, yet still romantic palette is applied to the upstairs rooms. The furniture here is mainly French, but with touches of wit and whimsy that are effective in conveying the residents' appreciation of a variety of styles and their informed sense of humor.

Carl D'Aquino/Geordi Humphreys Interior Designers   **Pieter Estersohn** Photographer

TROPICAL SPLENDOR

Palm Beach, Florida • 1,600 square feet/149 square meters • design budget: not disclosed

Most of the furnishings were rescued from local thrift shops. Many of the fabrics are 1950s-era period documents, found at flea markets and secondhand shops around the world. The residence itself, a rather nondescript, 1950s cinderblock and stucco Florida house, was transformed into a sunny, colorful, and whimsical reflection of the owner's design sensibility and tongue-in-cheek attitude.

Working closely with Manhattan-based interior designer Carl D'Aquino, the client was able to create a big impression on a tightly controlled budget. The recycled furnishings were given a fresh coat of paint or refinished to pristine condition. Original details within the house, such as tidewater cypress paneling, were beautifully restored. What was once old has become new again.

A fresh and newfangled kind of minimalism, employing extravagant and often fairly baroque elements, is achieved. Clutter is avoided at all costs, with excessive flourishes kept to the minimum. There's an inherent appreciation of the lines and forms of the vintage furniture and objects incorporated.

Plenty of Florida sunshine pours into the summery interiors of the Palm Beach home of an avid collector of vintage 1950s furniture, art, and decorative objects. In keeping with the period, wooden Venetian blinds cover some of the windows, but most are left bare. All the colors of the house, inside and out, are inspired by the sea, says interior designer Carl D'Aquino.

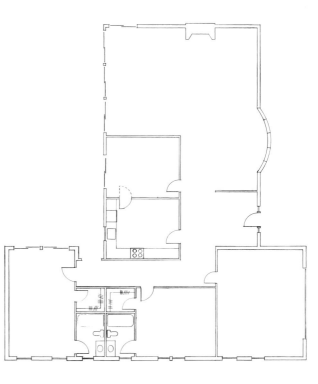

Benjamin Noriega-Ortiz Interior Designer   ✚   **Peter Margonelli** Photographer

CALMING EFFECT

Amagansett, New York • 1,200 square feet/112 square meters • design budget: not disclosed

When Rene Fuentes-Chao and Manhattan interior designer Benjamin Noriega-Ortiz bought their own weekend house in Amagansett, New York, their first instinct was to open up the existing space. Their initial renovation involved the removal of a series of smaller, boxy rooms in order to create a large, open living/dining space with access to the outdoor deck, pool area, and garden.

They clothed this multifunctional central area of the house, with its relatively soaring ceilings, in neutral tones, with sea-foam green upholstered pieces punctuating the space for an overall soothing spatial experience. Simple cottons and parachute fabrics were used throughout for easy maintenance, according to the pair. While some furniture was custom-made, the more serious pieces are combined with antiques and objects of interest found at flea markets. "Nothing too expensive," remarks Noriega-Ortiz, of his collected wares. Also on hand are some contemporary classics. Decades of style are blended in a fresh, unassuming, and ultimately satisfying method. It's a case study that isn't too studied.

67

The mélange of styles, periods, shapes, and textures within the Amagansett residence of Rene Fuentes-Chao and Benjamin Noriega-Ortiz is made harmonious through the use of a muted, but not monochromatic, palette applied to all surfaces within the space. No overhead lighting was allowed, only metal table lamps, which give off a softer light, have been used.

A sense of openness pervades every room of the house, which is fully furnished, but does not have any feeling of being over-stuffed. The whirlpool bath, an especially luxurious addition to the house, is positioned within a pavilion-like structure overlooking the pool area.

Mimmi O'Connell Interior Designer ▓ **Fritz von der Schulenburg/The Interior Archive** Photographer

SIMPLE PLEASURES

Tuscany, Italy • 6,000 square feet/557 square meters • design budget: not disclosed

The architecture of a Tuscan-style farmhouse in the rolling countryside outside of Siena is its strongest suit. British designer Mimmi O'Connell recognized this immediately, and minimally embellished the spectacular spaces within the residence to produce a crisp, clean ambiance in which the furnishings enhance the effect of the interior architecture rather than compete with it.

The sculptural quality of plaster walls throughout the house provide a subtly patterned and textured backdrop, which is enlivened when struck by light. Many of the windows are left untreated, allowing for unobstructed transmission of light. Pull-down shades are seen in some rooms, installed for privacy and practicality. When curtains appear, they are of a simple drapey variety, pulled back to allow inhabitants to take in the lovely views of the surrounding countryside.

Furnishings are kept to an absolute minimum and are not complex designs that draw too much attention or make too much of a statement. Fabrics are elegant and simple — O'Connell has a preference for old faded Ottoman textiles, eighteenth-century French embroidered silks, Indian and Persian designs, linens, and mattress ticking. There is a certain splendor in the harmony produced, that is in keeping with the surroundings, yet comfortable and unpretentious.

The main living/entertaining spaces in this Tuscan farmhouse offer plenty of comfortable seating, good lighting by day and in the evening, and places where conversation is encouraged. Walls are left bare; floors, when covered, are done so with the simplest sisal area rugs; windows are untreated.

While furnished minimally, comfort is always a consideration for O'Connell, who likes to counter strict geometry with soft and supple elements. There is a timeless quality to the interiors of the farmhouse, which does not resort to the use of clichés.

Furniture pieces, a very select number of artworks, and objects on display were chosen for their quality. The texture of the plaster walls throughout the house is activated by light.

ROWDY SERENITY

Southern Maine • 9,000 square feet/836 square meters • design budget: not disclosed

Investing the new with the old without appearing stodgy is a difficult proposition. Washington, D.C.-based interior designer Mary Douglas Drysdale approached this coastal Maine property — a newly built and generously scaled shingle-style house—by embracing the past, using classical American elements in a fresh way. "I see myself as a new traditionalist," she explains. "Correct proportions and serious detailing are important to me, but too much formality can be disturbing…Spaces need to be designed to make people feel at ease."

Drysdale distributed elements so that each can be appreciated individually, but can also interact within the whole. Achieving the right balance between forms, and arranging pieces in vignettes that have visual depth, gives each room a clear sense of place. Each bedroom, for instance, is given a unique fabric treatment that distinguishes it enough to refer to each room by a particular name: the green room, the buffalo plaid room, the bee room.

Old things are given a bit of punch; the primarily antique furnishings are revved up with daring fabric treatments and an adventurous, though refined, color scheme. A few rescues were performed, such as the elegant dining room table, which was originally finished in a dullish orange and brown. Stripped, painted, and glazed in antique white with a series of hand-painted gray starfish on board, the table was transformed from its carbuncle status.

81

"Plaid is the stripe of the nineties. It reflects a level of formality in a relaxed way," remarks interior designer Mary Douglas Drysdale, who formulated the interiors of a new coastal Maine cottage by mixing periods and styles, within a context that provides a smooth transition between pieces — no jumble! She's put the emphasis on the integrity of each element.

In the otherwise very tailored
master bedroom, brightly colored patterns are introduced
for a livelier, relaxed impact.
The furniture is a mix of
antiques found mostly in
Maine and new designs by
Mary Douglas Drysdale. An
extensive program of stenciling
— a throwback to traditional
American practices — is
adopted in the Maine house,
on walls, furnishings, and
fabrics. The wainscoting and
tile floors in the master bathroom harken back to a gentler
era in a room that addresses
contemporary needs. Win-
dow treatments are kept
simple to allow for views out
to the Atlantic.

Juan Montoya Interior Designer ✜ **Tuca Reinés** Photographer

TROPICAL SUITE

Miami Beach, Florida • 1,500 square feet/39 square meters • design budget: not disclosed

One can get carried away with the idea of regionalism. While context is an important consideration, one wouldn't want to make a too jarring or startlingly inappropriate statement.

There is something to be said for spaces that are not overly thematic. And a more personal statement is made through an environment that doesn't seem too programmed or "perfect."

This Miami Beach apartment takes many cues from its location in an Art Deco-style building. In addition, there is a texture to the apartment that's due to a coherently mingled range of styles.

Everything is in accord, with a completely contemporary sense to the presentation. The overall effect cannot be labeled. Included are elements that incorporate the concept of a 1950s tropical paradise, as well as several nineteenth-century English and Irish pieces, African and Asian artifacts, and Montoya's own designs. All are blended not only for surprise, but to build a unified reflection of the individual's eclectic tastes, talents, and varied interests.

Lighting is located along the perimeters of the rooms to provide ambient light and to highlight the architecture of the spaces. No rules or specific elements dominate the look of the Miami Beach apartment. Colors are used to "define zones of activity, e.g., dining, sleeping, etc.," says the designer, adding that "color is also used to enhance the sculptural qualities of the furniture."

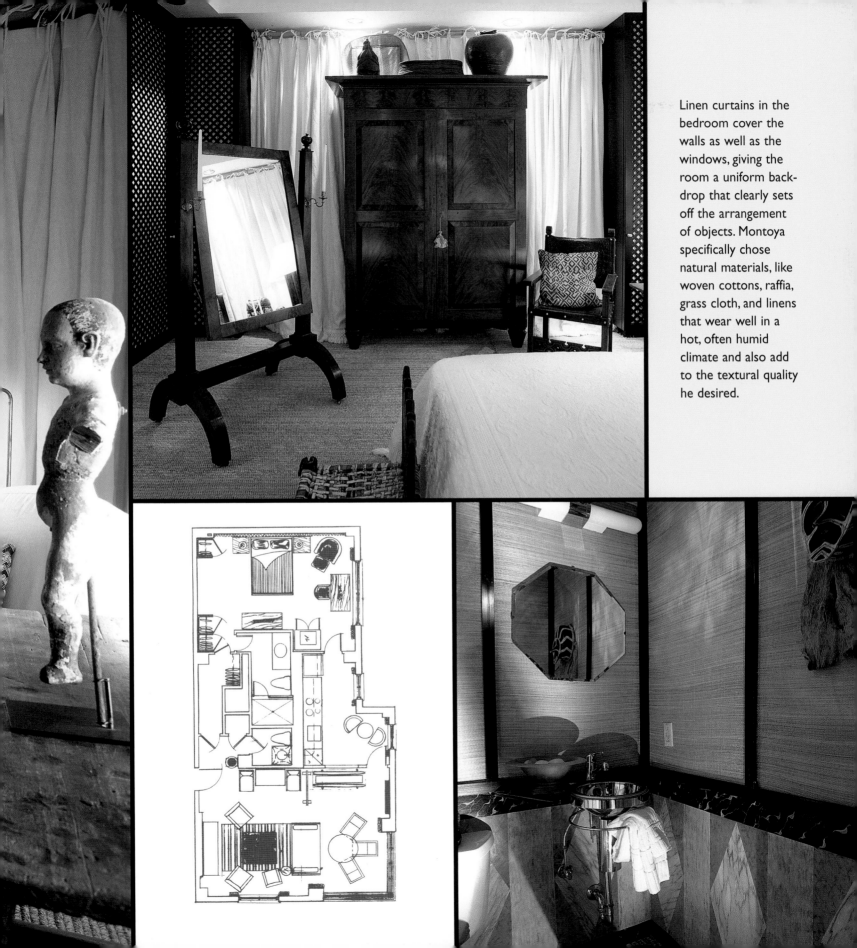

Linen curtains in the bedroom cover the walls as well as the windows, giving the room a uniform backdrop that clearly sets off the arrangement of objects. Montoya specifically chose natural materials, like woven cottons, raffia, grass cloth, and linens that wear well in a hot, often humid climate and also add to the textural quality he desired.

Paul Siskin Interior Designer   ■■   **Fernando Bengoechea** Photographer

DEVELOPING TASTE

Metropolitan New York • 2,000 square feet/186 square meters • design budget: $150,000

Out with the chintz, the bows, the fussiness. In with the concepts of restraint, elegance, quiet luxury, and freshness. Interior designer Paul Siskin followed the request of his clients, a young couple who didn't want anything too precise. He stayed away from busyness, developing a palette that's relatively free of patterns, with an overall blue-and-camel color scheme which evolved from the coloration of the fine carpet selected for the living room.

In terms of collecting, "the clients are just starting out," explains Siskin, and the rooms, designed to be gradually filled over a lifetime, are a base from which to grow. For now, however, they offer a quasi-traditional atmosphere, suitable for casual entertaining, and comfortable for relaxation. The home presents the kind of sophisticated, and timeless appearance associated with urban living.

Siskin's expert eye is apparent in the selection of the furnishings. Rooms are pared down without a sense of anything missing. The dining room doubles as a study and an extension of the entry gallery.

Window treatments are traditional silk-and-satin tie-back curtains that lend a softening texture in the master bedroom. A layer of sheers conceals the view, which did not play a big part in the realization of the scheme, according to Siskin. He describes the surrounding landscape as "real urban" (while the apartment does have an oblique view of a park, the majority of its windows face the building across the street).

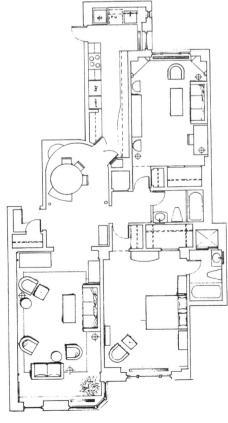

Sig Bergamin Architect/Interior Designer   **Tuca Reinés** Photographer

MIX MASTER

Campos Do Jordão, Brazil • 754 square feet/70 square meters • design budget: $10,000

It was the American architectural theorist Robert Venturi who coined the phrase "less is a bore" in response to the strict and controlled aesthetic of International Style Modernism. Bringing disparate elements together successfully is a tremendous challenge, but lives generally are not so focused as to allow for commitments to one particular style, color, or even a particular pattern. Designer Sig Bergamin's country retreat outside São Paulo offers an alternative to the "just paint everything white and it will go together" school of thought.

Instead of playing the match game, he collected all the leftovers from his former places and celebrated their differences, layering pattern upon pattern, color upon color, texture upon texture. Leopard meets paisley meets floral. The result: an exceedingly harmonious and cozy nest. There's a method to the madness.

To Bergamin, simple is not minimal. Visual comfort comes from the familiar. He surrounds himself with the possessions he loves, most of which he's lived with for many years. In that sense, too much is never enough.

Flowers are a pervasive decorative element throughout the house — a nod to the surrounding pastoral landscape. Most of the furnishings and works of art in the cottage were collected over the years from flea markets around the world.

In the master bedroom, a favorite plaid wallpaper is used as a solid ground against which cherished items are positioned.

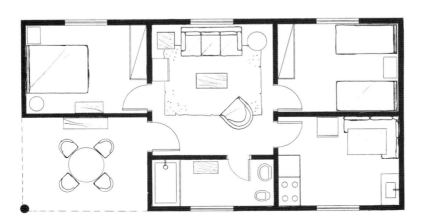

David H. Mitchell Interior Designer ❖ **Walter Smalling** Photographer

Dot Matrix

Western Maryland • 1,200 square feet / 111 square meters • design budget: $100,000

C haracter is hard to come by. Without resorting to cuteness, designer David H. Mitchell of Washington, D.C., created a family-oriented space in a Maryland house that has a personality reflective of its owners/users, and that makes a decorative statement that won't get stale with time. "Decoration for pure decoration sake is no longer valid," says the designer of the wooden balls positioned "whimsically" across the crown moldings in the space. "The balls were added to give a relationship to other strong wood pieces used," he explains, further noting that he "rescued" an item that would have probably ended up on the scrap pile.

Visual comfort and balance are not the only aspects emphasized in the project, a two-room space that seems more like one, due to the strong bit of aesthetic joinery that prevails. "The room is set up so that the fireplace is the central element in the main seating area, but there are still other intimate and private spaces within the room," states Mitchell. "The flow and placement of furniture makes it conducive to moving through the space without obstacles," adds the designer. And when one does decide to settle someplace, the cushions of upholstered pieces are stuffed with soft down to cradle and comfort the sitter. It's from this aspect that one is able to admire the highlighted collection of found objects and architectural elements on display.

Linen, cotton, and wool upholstery is played off against natural textures such as stone and wood in a Maryland sitting/ dining room designed by David H. Mitchell of Washington, D.C. A custom-designed cup- board holds television and video equipment handsomely in the space intended for multipurpose family use. Modern accents are mixed with the traditional as well as the tongue-in-cheek.

Sam Robin Interior Designer ■ **Daniel Aubry** Photographer

SOUTHERN SPICE

Southeastern Florida • 13,000 square feet/1207 square meters • design budget: not disclosed

The romance of North Africa and the Mediterranean were imported to this South Florida neighborhood. Interior designer Sam Robin created a new-style fantasy environment, with an emphasis on textures and strong color statements. "Originally, the owners wanted something contemporary on their waterfront property," Robin explains, and then she took

them to see a Miami Beach restaurant she'd designed in a fantastical Middle Eastern vernacular style. So long sleek. After that exposure, they were hooked, and started traveling with their designer to Morocco, picking up a rich array of handcrafted elements that have become the basis of an amazing collection that they live with every day.

Inherent in Robin's design approach is the blending of ingredients within a structure that is ultimately simple and pure. Some rooms have a more formal flavor. Some are clean and spare, while others offer multiple layers. "It's a three-story place, but all the rooms are on a human scale," states the designer.

There's a certain freedom, a contemporary take on a theme that's remarkably at home in this tropical environment. On the practical side, the construction of this style of house included an added bonus: its thick walls keep the interiors comfortably cool, even during the most sultry months of the year.

East meets West in the three-story residence where patterns and textures are used in a restrained fashion to avoid too much of a Casbah look. The interiors offer a fresh interpretation of a historic style.

Robin selected and mixed exotic elements imported from throughout the Mediterranean world and the Near East, as well as India, to create a comfortably eclectic mix, with each space in the house possessing a particular character. Some spaces, such as the dining room, have a more formal and elegant look, achieved by the introduction of richly colored and textured fabrics, fine woods, and deeply toned, mottled walls.

High drama comes into play, but in a restrained fashion. The rooms are fairly simple, with architectural detailing a paramount concern. Off-white walls were given the patina of age by washing them with pigments and flat beer, according to interior designer Sam Robin.

Jean-Louis Ménard Interior Designer   ᠙᠙   **Peter Margonelli** Photographer

ACUTE ACCENT

New York, New York • 3,000 square feet/279 square meters • design budget: not disclosed

Imported styles often lose something in the translation. This is not the case in the spacious New York City apartment of design editor Suzanne Slesin and writer Michael Steinberg, both of whom are avowed Francophiles. The couple called upon Parisian interior architect

Jean-Louis Ménard to invest their home with a hybrid French atmosphere, not re-create the clichéd Versailles-on-the-Hudson look. The apartment is invested with a style all its own, reflective of its owners' varied interests and quirky aesthetic.

Slesin and Steinberg are more interested in French vernacular than the noble Louis or fancy Rothschild style. The pure colors of Provence, bistro culture, the discreet charm of the bourgeoisie, so to speak, are more their speed. Ménard heeded their call, without over-doing it, as they are more than one-style kind of people. They are also avid collectors of folk art and contemporary paintings and furniture from a variety of places beyond the borders of France. With Ménard, the couple was able to fully integrate their personal style and design preferences in a comfortably layered, well textured, and delectably juxtaposed mode.

A sense of permanence pervades the casually arranged rooms of this New York City apartment, renovated by interior architect Jean-Louis Ménard with a hybrid French accent. The dining room, decorated in British fashion, also serves as a library and study. With collector-clients as zealous as Slesin and Steinberg (they have pieces of various origin — Jamaica, Great Britain, France, the United States — from the antique to the contemporary), Ménard had a free hand in integrating their cherished belongings, creating wonderful juxtapositions of forms.

Vicente Wolf Interior Designer ❖ **Vicente Wolf** Photographer

COOL WORLD

Metropolitan New York • 3,000 square feet/279 square meters • design budget: not disclosed

The renovation of this fairly undistinguished house overlooking the Atlantic Ocean into a stylish, airy, and extremely tailored, yet ultimately comfortable retreat took several years of gradual recomposition. "My focus was the sea," explains Manhattan interior designer Vicente Wolf, when talking about the decoration of his weekend house. "Thus, I maintained a very simple palette and floor plan."

Wolf incorporated a fairly diverse range of meaningful objects and furnishings collected during his travels over the years. "Some antiques are from England, India, and France," he says, but they are mixed in with pieces from the 1940s and 1950s for a cleaner, simpler, friendlier character. The overall look "incorporates the past in a modern, stylish way," he explains.

The house is best described as smooth and integrated, with a practical bent which, at first sight, is not apparent. Floors throughout are stone, but their natural color exudes warmth. All furniture is slipcovered for easy cleaning or replacement. The scale of things is paramount, providing visual as well as physical comfort.

122

A sense of lightness, due not only to the extensive use of white fabric, is innate within the confines of interior designer Vicente Wolf's weekend residence. The antique is accompanied by the modern, with the majority of the upholstered pieces designed by Wolf himself. The house's décor is admittedly programmed, but there is a casualness inherent within the structure.

Mimmi O'Connell Interior Designer ■ **Fritz von der Schulenburg/The Interior Archive** Photographer

UNCOMMON SENSE

London, England • 3,000 square feet/279 square meters • design budget: not disclosed

A West London flat designed by British interiors expert Mimmi O'Connell is anything but. The essence of a successful residential interior? In O'Connell's opinion it's "the perfect eclectic mixture of old, sometimes precious, and new, with lights that can be dimmed to enhance a room and the people living in it."

Comfort is an overriding factor that contributes to the success of the apartment's interior scheme. Deep-cushioned sofas, chaise lounges, large stools and ottomans, and roomy English-style armchairs are O'Connell's means of achieving an excessive level of comfort. She says her craving for comfort is common sense: "You want places where you can sit comfortably and relax with family and friends. You want beds that are dreamy, where you will relax and spend a really good time!"

Throughout the London flat an elegant, layered effect is achieved. Textures play against one another in a well-syncopated rhythm, while patterns that might seemingly clash work together to create a visually coherent impact. The traditional rules concerning what works well together, and that only two or three fabrics at the most can be used in a single room are decidedly broken. Ethnic pieces coexist with traditional European furnishings, but the "curio-shop look" is avoided, through the exercise of some restraint. Too much can be enough, but a skilled designer/editor with an impeccable eye for detail can bring it all together in a way that is fresh and livable.

The mélange of new and old-world items from a variety of cultures, ensconced within rooms that offer numerous plays between textures and patterns, adds a comforting human touch to this London flat.

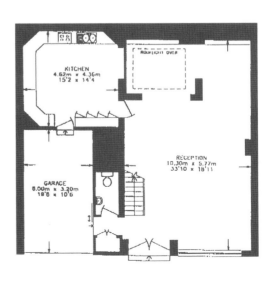

O'Connell advises the purchase of good pieces of furniture — "They are yours for life, and for children and grandchildren." She believes that it's the details that make houses wonderfully comfortable: crisp linen sheets, lots of pillows in bedrooms, piles of white towels in bathrooms, scented rooms, flowers, and books.

Laura Bohn Interior Designer   &G   **Peter Margonelli** Photographer

FRESH ANTIQUITY

Erwinna, Pennsylvania • 3,500 square feet/325 square meters • design budget: not disclosed

Outside, the 200-year-old rural Pennsylvania house is the quintessential moss-covered farmhouse, with stones jutting through plaster and peeling paint left as they've come to be. Inside, designer Laura Bohn, of LBDA Design Associates in New York, has considerably freshened up, while maintaining a respectful and subtle hand.

Antiques are mixed with contemporary pieces against a muted, textural backdrop that is made crisper and more tailored by painting architectural details, such as window moldings, white. There are no window treatments, and as the property is fairly secluded and the issue of privacy did not come into play, Bohn was able to emphasize the pure details of the original windows.

The furnishings on hand present a varied mixture of tastes, from Shaker and early American pieces to contemporary. These have been collected from local flea markets, antique shows, auctions, and dealers. The attitude is definitely a modern one, with the choice of pieces informed by the guiding principle of clean lines.

"Most Americans have a nostalgia for the old, the worn, the used, and a yearning for the past" says designer Laura Bohn. In designing the interiors of her rural Pennsylvania farmhouse, she has a clear esteem for the centuries-old context of the property, but hasn't succumbed to the idea of banning the present. The mix of old and new addresses the need for comfort and function.

The house possesses a new kind of modernity
that incorporates the warmth of old things while
engaging the practicality of contemporary life.

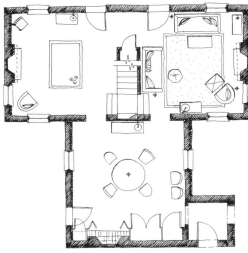

The soothing rooms are filled with a number of personal collections, including bird's nests found around the area, buttons (which Bohn glues to picture frames), wooden boxes, architectural artifacts, brown glass bottles, and American pottery.

Joan Weissman Interior Designer ✤ **©Alexander Vertikoff/Jack Parsons** Photographers

PRIDE OF PLACE

Central New Mexico • 300 square feet/28 square meters • design budget: not disclosed

The modest adobe-style house in New Mexico, where talented custom rug designer and ceramist Joan Weissman resides, was built in 1928. Weissman worked with local architect Robert E. Strell to restore the house. They enhanced the existing landscape by creating a new guest room and bathroom while maintaining the structure's original details.

The house is filled with examples of Weissman's work, for an especially personal expression. Also incorporated are many items from India that the artist amassed, as well as a fine collection of quilts and textiles. The clichés of the "packaged" South-western look are avoided.

There's a rich mixture of contemporary and antique: turn-of-the-century furniture, Native American art, items from the Indian subcontinent, and many new items. Spaces are filled sparingly and logically. Each corner of the house can be compared to a still life, with objects and furniture positioned neatly and artfully in a balanced and restrained fashion. There's no sensory overload. Everything is carefully blended.

While thoroughly updated, many elements of the original 1928 kitchen were retained. Throughout the house, colorful rugs and ceramic works created by the owner are on display.

All rug designs © **Joan Weissman**

Benjamin Noriega-Ortiz Interior Designer ▦ **Peter Margonelli** Photographer

EASY FLAIR

Metropolitan New York • 1,400 square feet/130 square meters • design budget: not disclosed

his weekend retreat is in a choice location for sophisticated New Yorkers who wish to escape their harried Monday-through-Friday routines. The area offers the unique combination of a rural country-life atmosphere and a New England-style seaside ambiance.

Once primarily a summer resort area, city dwellers have come to appreciate the seasonal changes, settling in year round. The contemporary beach cottage is a versatile environment, geared for year-round use. New York City-based interior designer Benjamin Noriega-Ortiz gives the house a cool, rather minimal appearance, using natural woods, interior wainscoting, comfy furnishings, and a big stone fireplace. This sparing, but effective treatment removes any feeling of coldness during the harsher winter months.

Touches of sea-foam green, which acknowledge the house's proximity to the shore, invigorate the primarily white interiors of the house. White-canvas Roman shades on windows are Noriega-Ortiz's simple solution, flooding rooms with light during daylight hours, if so desired. Bleached wood floors are not diluted with carpets; walls are fairly bare. Old and new furnishings, some reinvented with a coat of paint, blend to show each piece off to its best advantage.

A cooled-down palette is employed by designer Benjamin Noriega-Ortiz for this weekend refuge. The play between sleek and soft, smooth and tactile, creates a subtly comfortable interior climate that's favorable throughout the year and adaptable to seasonal changes.

Private spaces are sheathed in traditional wainscotting, recalling historical cottage interiors found all along the Eastern Seaboard. Modern lamps and accessories are used in conjunction with warm wooden antique furniture. The hybrid quality of the design scheme gives it a truly contemporary, but not dated, appearance.

Stephen Sills/James Huniford Interior Designers ❦ **Thibault Jeanson** Photographer

FREE RANGE

Metropolitan New York • 1,500 square feet/140 square meters • design budget: not disclosed

W hen things match too much, change is in order. Contradictions, furthermore, can be fascinating as well as amicable. There's a kind of joy to going against the tide, challenging the notions of what's generally considered correct, tasteful, or safe. When a new breed of dialogue between elements is established, a distinct language is wrought. Louis XVI can converse over the centuries with Jean-Michel Frank. Great extravagance can meet the humble, at least halfway. A compromise? Not at all.

Partners in decorating, Stephen Sills and James Huniford of Manhattan, conceived a very special guest house. Within its walls, which are colored, patinated, and detailed to seem "a hundred-years old," according to Huniford, and against its stone and sea-grass-covered floors, there is a playful disregard for so-called rules. Form doesn't necessarily follow function; all the furnishings are considered to be in the realm of accessories and there is no hierarchical order enforced. Benches serve as chairs, for example, and chairs are "objects."

An exuberant, charming environment is ultimately established, which is not bogged down by the past and celebrates its forms and contributions. Calmness too is part of the formula. The heavy hand was played out long ago. The whole space is a collection, "rooted in the wide, free-ranging mindset characteristic of Americans at their best," states Huniford.

Contrasts and contradictions give the rooms of the guest house a surprisingly rich effect, but one that doesn't take too much too seriously. While the many layers, periods, and forms could border on pastiche, there's a certain strength, a sophisticated viewpoint, and a sense of restraint inherent in the scheme that exalts many eras and tastes by combining them as one in lieu of placing each on a pedestal.

René Fernandes Filho Interior Designer   ✚   **João Ribeiro** Photographer

TACTILE TASTE

São Paulo, Brazil • 1,356 square feet / 126 square meters • design budget: $20,000

B razilian architect/interior designer René Fernandes Filho cooked up a professional chef's São Paulo residence which is appropriately flavored with elements from many nations — "Much like the melting-pot culture of Brazil itself," the designer explains. Mixed together in a manner that is casual and highly colorful, with an emphasis on extending the rooms of the house into the large and lushly planted tropical garden, are ingredients from Asia, Africa, Portugal, and France, as well as local homegrown art and artifacts.

Both physical and visual comfort are key in the house, which was renovated and redecorated on a fairly small budget. Softer upholstered pieces, pillows of various sizes and shapes, and sculptural furnishings provide a contrast to the more angular geometry of the house as well as to some of the heavier traditional furniture pieces, in the possession of the owner's family for generations. Shards of tile are positioned in irregular patterns framing doorways and as a new-style wainscoting, bringing further depth to the tactile environment.

The décor of the house is a mélange that works because, at its heart, the arrangements are quite structured. Slick is countered with rough; the old-fashioned confronts the newfangled; hot meets cool; and formal coexists with casual. It's a warm and very friendly place that captures the personality of the individual who resides there.

A relatively bright palette throughout the project, and the use of various surface textures, including bamboo poles, stucco, stone, concrete, and wood bring a lively and fascinating rhythm to the eclectically decorated interior and outdoor rooms of this São Paulo residence.

Celeste B. Cooper ASID Interior Designer ▪▪ **Richard Mandelkorn** Photographer

HIGH CONTRAST

Weston, Massachusetts • 3,500 square feet/325 square meters • design budget: not disclosed

An existing suburban house doesn't have to look "suburban." Such is the case with a house designed by Celeste B. Cooper for a couple in the semirural suburb of Weston, Massachusetts, approximately ten miles from downtown Boston.

A spare, but sophisticated aesthetic was adopted for the decoration program of the residence. A tailored black-and-cream palette is applied throughout the various rooms of the house in a manner that is subtle, yet effective. In design circles, the concept of coordination has come to have fairly negative connotations, but here Cooper has gone beyond simple "match" tactics to create a series of spaces that are soothingly integrated and blend well together as one moves through them.

A generally contemporary style was embraced, but there is much warmth and an emphasis on bringing the outdoors inside, especially because there are no window treatments. Brightly colored furnishings and fabrics are used as punctuation marks in a number of instances, as means of "finishing" and balancing the overall impression of each space.

Though the majority of rooms in the house are furnished and finished in a restful combination of natural tones and black, colors and textures are used as highlights throughout several rooms in this decidedly "un-suburban" suburban residence. A more dramatic look is achieved in the entrance hall and stairwell, where brightly colored fixtures, fittings, furnishings, and fabrics provide a sharp contrast to the darkly painted walls and tiled and leopard-carpeted floors.

Mary Douglas Drysdale Interior Designer   **Andrew Lautman** Photographer

GRAND FUNK

Washington, D.C. • 3,000 square feet/279 square meters • design budget: not disclosed

"I like diversity," says interior designer Mary Douglas Drysdale. That statement alone explains her approach to the design of a Washington, D.C., artist's loft. The perfect balance between folksy and sleek, formal and casual, minimal and maximal, contemporary and ancient is achieved. The fact that seemingly contradictory items can be paired amuses and challenges her. "One has to work reasonably hard to achieve balance and symmetry when you do not have the actual thing," she admits.

The best way to handle this? For Drysdale, it's a matter of reigning things in, creating interesting juxtapositions of shapes, forms, angles, solids, and voids. Out with the superfluous. The preference is toward taking away rather than adding. Adopting a spare aesthetic, in which objects can be seen clearly, enhances their appearance and elevates each element's importance within the scheme. Things that seemingly wouldn't go together can harmonize. After all, opposites do attract more often than not.

"I find serenity in a well-ordered space," says designer Mary Douglas Drysdale, who also followed a less-is-more approach in creating the stark, yet light and warm interiors. Color is injected to liven up specific areas of the loft, which have an overall gallery-style atmosphere in which elements are carefully placed for optimal impact.

Furniture and works of art in the loft's various rooms are positioned so that their individual curves, lines, and forms can be seen fully. The light and airy atmosphere of the residence is assisted by the undressed windows, lending views of urban greenery outside.

Barbara Hauben-Ross Interior Designer ✤ **Billy Cunningham** Photographer

GRAND ALLUSION

New York, New York • 2,000 square feet/186 square meters • design budget: not disclosed

Interior designer Barbara Hauben-Ross once lived amid a sea of white on white. Her apartment on Manhattan's Upper West Side, where she has lived for over two decades, was given a more peaceful, less self-conscious mood, incorporating cherished pieces of furniture, decorative arts, and paintings. In fact, the majority of the furnishings were re-used in the new scheme, which has a rich European-influenced character.

Soft greens and natural beiges set the tone in the space. Textured fabrics lend patterns to the design, which are kept subtle to complement the neutral background.

The wide variety of furnishings employed include examples of the French and German Art Deco era, 1970s Italian pieces, formerly white laminate-sheathed end tables that are decoratively painted to look like rosewood, as well as some designs by Hauben-Ross, such as the dining and coffee tables. The mix brings an array of elements together in order to create what she defines as a degree of much-desired coziness.

In this Manhattan apartment, periods and cultures are blended to present an elegant, yet comfortable and highly personal statement. Fulper and Niloak pottery, sleek Italian chairs, Art Deco and Wiener Werkstätte pieces, among other elements, are incorporated into the scheme. Natural-colored sisal covers the floors in the living room. Walls are painted a soft green. Decorative ceiling moldings, restored to pristine condition, are original to the apartment, built in 1912.

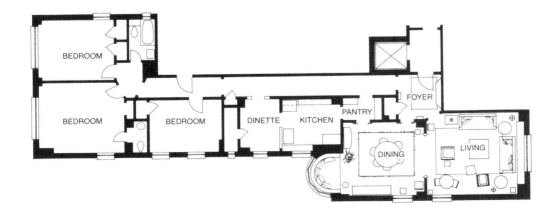

BEDROOM

BEDROOM

BEDROOM

DINETTE

KITCHEN

PANTRY

FOYER

DINING

LIVING

DIRECTORY

Repertoire
Celeste B. Cooper, ASID
560 Harrison Avenue
Boston, Massachussetts 02118
United States
Tel: (617) 426-3865
Fax: (617) 426-1879

Repertoire
Celeste B. Cooper, ASID
325 East 57th Street
New York, New York 10022
United States
Tel: (212) 826-5667
Fax: (212) 935-7926

Ronald Bricke & Associates, Inc.
Ronald Bricke
333 East 69th Street, #7B
New York, New York 10021
United States
Tel: (212) 472-9006
Fax: (212) 472-9008

Sam Robin Interior Design
Sam Robin
1000 Venetian Way, #112
Miami, Florida 33186
United States
Tel: (305) 375-0727
Fax: (305) 375-8189

Sig Bergamin Interiors
Sig Bergamin
20 East 69th Street, #3C
New York, New York 10021
United States
Tel: (212) 861-4515
Fax: (212) 861-3667

Siskin Valls, Inc.
Paul Siskin
21 West 58th Street
New York, New York 10019
United States
Tel: (212) 752-3790
Fax: (212) 752-3935

Solis Betancourt
Jose Solis Betancourt
Paul M. Sherrill
1054 Potomac Street, N.W.
Washington, D.C. 20007
United States
Tel: (202) 659-8734
Fax: (202) 659-0035

Stephen Sills Associates
Stephen Sills
James Huniford
30 East 67th Street
New York, New York 10021
United States
Tel: (212) 988-1636
Fax: (212) 988-2006

Strell Design
Robert E. Strell
120 Morningside Drive, S.E.
Albuquerque, New Mexico 87108
United States
Tel: (505) 268-2321
Fax: (505) 268-2328

Strohl & Company
Mike Strohl
150 West 25th Street
New York, New York 10001
United States
Tel: (212) 242-7200
Fax: (212) 242-1850

Vicente Wolf Associates, Inc.
Vicente Wolf
333 West 39th Street
New York, New York 10018
United States
Tel: (212) 465-0590
Fax: (212) 465-0639

PHOTOGRAPHERS

Alexander Vertikoff Photography
Alexander Vertikoff
P.O. Box 2079
Tijeras, New Mexico 87059
United States
Tel: (505) 281-7489

Daniel Aubry
365 First Avenue
New York, New York 10010
United States
Tel: (212) 598-4191
Fax: (212) 505-7670

Fernando Bengoechea
404 East 51st Street, #3A
New York, New York 10022
United States
Tel: (212) 754-2187

Brian Vanden Brink
P.O. Box 419
Rockport, Maine 04856
United States
Tel: (207) 236-4035
Fax: (207) 236-0704

Rob Brinson
887-B West Marietta Street
Atlanta, Georgia 30318
United States
Tel: (404) 874-2497
Fax: (404) 874-9666

Billy Cunningham
140 Seventh Avenue, #4C
New York, New York 10011
United States
Tel: (212) 429-6313
Fax: (212) 429-6313

Pieter Estersohn
Lachapelle Representation, Ltd.
420 East 54th Street, #14F
New York, New York 10022
United States
Tel: (212) 838-3170
Fax: (212) 758-6159

Michael L. Hill
Box 67, R.D.1
Chester, New York 10918
United States
Tel: (212) 734-5997
Fax: (212) 734-5997

The Interior Archive, Ltd.
    Fritz von der Shulenburg
7 Chelsea Studios
410 Fulham Road
London, England SW6-1EB
Tel: 0171-370-0595
Fax: 385-5403

Thibault Jeanson
310 West 99th Street, #802
New York, New York 10025
United States
Tel: (212) 316-7625
Fax: (212) 961-0284

Lautman Photography
    Andrew Lautman
4906 41st Street, N.W.
Washington, D.C. 20016
United States
Tel: (202) 966-2800
Fax: (202) 966-4240

Peter Margonelli
20 Desbrosses Street
New York, New York 10013
United States
Tel: (212) 941-0380
Fax: (212) 334-4449

Jack Parsons
1516A Pacheco Street
Santa Fe, New Mexico 87505
United States
Tel: (505) 984-8092
Fax: (505) 984-8092

Tuca Reinés
Rua Emanuel Kant, 58
São Paulo, São Paulo
Brazil 04536-050
Tel: 55-11-30619127
Fax: 55-11-8528735

João Ribeiro
Contraste Foto Imagem
Rua Drausio 466
São Paulo, São Paulo
Brazil 05511-010
Tel: 55-14-97247381

RSMP
Richard Mandelkorn
65 Beaver Pond Road
Lincoln, Massachussetts 01773
United States
Tel: (617) 259-3310
Fax: (617) 259-3312

Tim Street-Porter
2074 Watsonia Terrace
Los Angeles, California 90068
United States
Tel: (213) 874-4278

Vicente Wolf Associates, Inc.
    Vicente Wolf
333 West 39th Street
New York, New York 10018
United States
Tel: (212) 465-0590
Fax: (212) 465-0639

Walter Smalling Photography
    Walter Smalling
1541 8th Street, N.W.
Washington, D.C. 20001
United States
Tel: (202) 234-2438

INDEX

ACKNOWLEDGMENTS

My heartfelt thanks to all who contributed their time, resources and wisdom to *New American Style* including the staff of PBC International, Inc., Alice Martell, Karen Fisher, Suzanne Slesin, Olivia Buehl, Chapin Clark, Jennifer Talbott, John R. Snyder, Donna Paul, Linda Lachapelle, and all of the designers and photographers whose work appears in these pages.